The Great
DELI COOKBOOK

The Great DELI COOKBOOK

an adventure not equaled in modern gastronomy

PRODUCED AND WRITTEN BY
MERLE HORWITZ

RECIPES COURTESY
MARVIN SAUL
of
Junior's Deli of West Los Angeles
Billy Lowder – Executive Chef

ADDITIONAL TEXT BY
Mitchell Gamson

ORIGINAL PAINTINGS AND COVER BY
Carmel O'Mara

PRODUCTION BY
John Robinson and Allwyn O'Mara

ISBN#1-882383-06-0

Produced and written by Merle Horwitz
Additional copy by Mitchell Gamson
Original Art by Carmel O'Mara
Design/Pre-press production
by John Robinson and Allwyn O'Mara

Printing and book producton
Graphics Management, Los Angeles

Printed in Hong Kong

ACKNOWLEDGMENTS

The job of a producer is to point at people thought to be best and ask, "Can **you** do this?" and then to point at the finished product and say, "See, I told you **we could do it.**"

The art work of Carmel O'Mara in this Volume 1 of a series of similar cookbooks is the best art work seen in any such endeavor. Don't even argue. You can find great photography in cookbooks. But great art—that's almost impossible to find. But here it is, in this little stand up cook-book. Indeed, there are substantial offers to purchase the original paintings from which the covers and sections were taken, all of which have been refused, as of this date. Carmel's ability to transcribe the mind's eye to the canvas is a very special gift.

Billy Lowder, the Executive Chef for one of the famous Los Angeles delicatessens was able to take his restaurant specialties and reduce them to home cooking size and yet retain the uniqueness of his recipes. "The thing to do," he kept saying, "is to keep the real flavors of the real stuff—the vegetables, the chickens and meats, and not lose it all in the processes." He has succeeded. Marvin Saul decided on the breadth and scope of the recipes and insured the perfection of the final result employing his fifty years of experience in the deli business.

Allwyn O'Mara, Carmel's mother, fortuitously, is a book binder of significant repute. She supervised the styles and "look" and such things as the paper and cover thickness of the final creation.

Finally, John Robinson, the printer, the stylist of the print medium, organized the pages and the fonts and rolled the words around the pictures and suggested this and that, all of which had a touch of genius within.

Mitch Gamson, ancient semi-comic, and others have contributed to the wonderful foolishness that makes this book both real, practical, beautiful, silly and great fun.

Merle H. Horwitz

TABLE OF CONTENTS

SPECIALTIES

SALADS

HOMEMADE SOUPS and SANDWICHES

VOLUPTUOUS

Old Fashioned
Stuffed Cabbage
Melt in your mouth.
A hunk of heaven.
— page 62 —

Traditional
Mushroom & Barley Soup
Made the old time way
with flavorful dried
mushrooms — page 48.

Homemade
Cheese Blintzes
The original
"Lighter than a Cloud"
— page 18 —

Glossary of Terms

Yiddish to English and commonly misunderstood terms carefully, accurately and concisely defined. Page 75

INTRODUCTION

"Deli" isn't what you think it is. No, it's not a restaurant where all those 5PM early bird geezers hang out, the ones who didn't get a face lift; it's not a Yiddish hang out, an Italian pizza parlor; it's not a lox and bagel emporium or English pub. It's not a place where foreigners congregate.

It's an American Gastronomic Institution! That means that your local *Delicatessen* belongs to everyone.

You get Penicillin soups for the flu and for your aches and pains; pastramis on rye the size of a house for the cure of the great American Depression Syndrome; and, at the same time, you get relief from every addiction known to humankind by injecting potato pancake molecules into those starved, anemic little low cholesterol kind. Plus, grilled cheese, enormous roast beef sandwiches, corned beef and cabbage dinners, caesar salads and scrambled eggs with luscious belly cut smoked salmon and sauteed onions! It's impossible to start your shrink session in a salt starved condition. You need a Kosher Dill Pickle first!

It's what El Paso doesn't do well, what Des Moines doesn't fully understand; it's what Topeka and Corpus Christi aren't quite sure of what it is. It's not Latino, it's not Chinese, it's not Polish, or German, or Russian, or British or French, or Greek Orthodox. **It's all of these.**

This book will teach America that everything isn't up to date everywhere, but that it can be. A Deli is an American invention, like semi-conductors, high density television. A good delicatessen conducts pleasure into the hum-drum lives of the rich and famous. It is impossible to continue a modern civilization, or enter into the new time zones of the twenty-first century, go to Mars, set up space stations—unless the Deli business is clearly understood and appreciated by all. We suggest, humbly, that this invention must not be usurped by the Japanese or Koreans, that it be kept sacrosanct (non-ethnic sacred), that trade wars must never erupt over the exporting of the Deli concept.

Consequently, this cookbook will never be exported. We will have the warehouses guarded by established members of the Daughters of the American Revolution, resurrect the House Un-American Activities Committee and otherwise establish the proper safeguards for this American Institution.

For those of you who are American or who want to be, or hope to be, you gotta have this cookbook!

Specialties

Corned Beef Hash

*W*hat's the best thing you can do on a rainy day, a cold and dreary day? I know what you're going to say—not that! You go to the deli and you sit in a corner and order a hot cup of tea and a gorgeous, steaming dish of corned beef hash with a sunny-side-up egg beaming at you like an August sun!

On these dreary days you need to re-create these moments of fun in your own kitchen, in your pajamas watching a gooey love story on the TV, devouring the wonder of it on a tray in your bed so you can reach over any time and get a good hand on your partner in this . . .Voluptuous Adventure.

Then, instead of kibbitzing a waitress who wouldn't give you more than the time of day, you nudge your partner—who, unfortunately, is still eating and which, alas, is the down side to all the wonders of . . . The Great Deli Cookbook.

INGREDIENTS, Serves 4

8 medium	**Potatoes,** peeled and diced in $1/2$ inch cubes
$1/2$ pound	**Corned Beef,** diced in $1/2$ inch cubes
$1/4$ cup	**Olive Oil**
1 large	**Onion,** finely diced
1 medium	**Crying Towel**
$1/2$ teaspoon	**Garlic Salt** (or to taste)
$1/2$ teaspoon	**Fresh Ground Pepper**

METHOD

■ Place vegetable steamer in large saucepan, add about 1/4 inch of water to the pot. Bring to a boil and reduce heat to a simmer.

■ Place potatoes in the steamer and simmer/steam for 5-6 minutes.

■ Place potatoes in a large bowl.

■ Toss diced corned beef into same bowl.

■ Pour oil into a large non-stick skillet and heat.

■ Saute onions until soft.

■ Add corned beef, potatoes and seasonings. Saute until potatoes are brown and crispy, about 10 minutes.

■ Serve the hash with a fried egg on top. A poached egg works well with this also.

Tzimmis

*T*here we were—alone. She gazed at me with mystery in her eyes as she undid one tiny bit of one garment at a time. Slowly. Achingly . . . a button. A little zip. Then a slide, a shiver. A little wriggle. A shoe flew into the air. Could this be? My life raced before my eyes. I am a male type person so I was in deep trouble. My children, my marriage. My tender sensibilities! Oh my goodness!

A strap came down, then one more. This was a very difficult time. What did she want of me? How should I respond?

"What do you want of me?" I asked, trembling. "Just tell me!"

Another button. Another slip and slide. The room seemed to go dark, to swirl before my feverish eyes. "What do you want of me?"

A step and a toss and another garment was gone. Did you see that move?—Sally Rand couldn't make that move. Then another. The final shoe. The last stocking. A this. A that.

My stomach began to ache. My head pounded. Wisps of steam curled from my ears.

One more time, I moaned, "Please, what do you want of me?"

Suddenly, naked before God and country—and me—She screamed, "Tzimmis! I want Tzimmis! I want Tzimmis! Tzimmis! Tzimmis!—Do you hear me? I want Tzimmis!"

When you make this recipe, I want you to dismiss these thoughts, these images. Forget it all. Just make the damn Tzimmis.

INGREDIENTS, Serves 6 – 8

2 cups	**Carrots,** grated into thin slices
2 medium	**Yams,** grated or sliced thin
1/2 cup	**Unsalted Butter** (or margarine)
1/2 teaspoon	**Nutmeg**
1/2 cup	**Sugar**
1/2 teaspoon	**Salt**
1 cup	**Prunes,** pitted and diced

METHOD

- Place all ingredients except prunes into large and heavy pot.
- Simmer for 45 – 50 minutes; add prunes at about the 30 minute mark. Stir every few minutes.
- Remove from heat for 5 minutes.
- Pour into deep serving dish. Serve.

The Best! *This side dish can garnish any holiday meal or take the place of your regular vegetable.*

Kasha Varnishkas

I had to have lunch at an old folks home recently. They call them "Retirement Hotels." Hilton doesn't need to worry about the competition. The lunch menu was Kasha Varnishkas and Jello. The dining room had an urgent scent which covered a multitude of unhappy and unrelated scents. As I sat in my assigned booth I looked around at my future trying to connect but not succeeding.

A frail, diminished lady, maybe ninety pounds at about four foot ten, translucent skin and watery blue eyes, smiled at me. She was quite alone at a large table for four. It was one of those smiles that came from deep in the past, some wonderful childhood recollection, a birthday party perhaps, one of those moments of divine inner joy. She fluttered her eyelids at me and said, "I used to make this dish. It's very difficult, you know . . . to get it just right. Did you know I used to do this? Of course you did. All my children loved it."

I smiled, denying nothing. All at once she drew stern—I had become her son, her favorite child. "Sandy," she said, a touch of tremulous pique in her voice, "You didn't say anything about it. You have to take some home. I'm not cooking anymore this week. Now come over here."

"In a minute. Just a minute," I lied.

"It's the onions," she continued. "And the bow-ties have to be just so."

Then she looked up at me for a long puzzled moment. For some reason that look hurt me, something crawling into my psyche from the deep past. I figured I had to go along. "Sandy?" She queried.

I replied "Yes M'am."

"Come here, Sandy, and give momma a kiss, sweetheart."

There was no way out of it. As I leaned over, one of the bulky attendants came by and spoke to the old girl. "Mizz Walbert," the attendant said, no smiles in her voice, "This isn't Sandy. He died, dear. Remember?"

They told me later that the doctors insist that the attendants be absolutely truthful with the residents, with very old people—bunch of baloney. Mizz Walbert brushed her off with a tiny wave of her fingers, leaned toward me and gave me a big hug and asked, "You liked the Kasha Varnishkas?"

"Wonderful. Great. Terrific. The best," I kept repeating as she was led away. I never saw her again and never asked.

I always think of that story when I order this dish at a good Deli. "The bowties have to be just so."

And your heart has to be in the right place.

INGREDIENTS, Serves 6 – 8

1 1/4 cups	**Bow Tie Noodles**
1 tablespoon	**Salt**
1 1/2 quarts	**Water**
1 teaspoon	**Margarine**

2 small	**Onions,** diced
1 whole	**Egg**
2 cups	**Kasha**
1/2 teaspoon	**White Pepper**
1/4 cup	**Salad Oil** (corn oil preferred)

METHOD

■ Cook the bow tie noodles in a little more than a quart of boiling water with 1/2 tablespoon salt about 8 minutes. Drain and set aside.

■ Saute onions in a separate large saute pan with 1 teaspoon of margarine and salad oil until golden.

■ Beat egg and set aside.

■ Add Kasha to onions in the saute pan. Add beaten egg and mix well and saute for an additional 2 minutes.

■ Add the kasha, onions and egg mixture to remaining water with salt and pepper. A good variation is to use a half can of chicken broth or a small cube of chicken bouillon added to the water instead of all water.

■ Cover. Simmer until water gone.

This recipe sometimes requires a little more water during the simmering process in order to make sure that Kasha is soft and fluffy. Just like rice, you have to keep the cover on the pot and still check the contents. This is impossible. However, "just do it."

Serve this dish in a small soup bowl or pasta dish with a cold borscht soup, with a side dish of a few sliced cucumbers flavored in wine vinegar and it's dinner or lunch fit for Presidents and Prime Ministers.

Noodle Kugle

*N*oodle kugle was invented by one Aram Delicatesse who resided in fifteenth century Czechoslovakia. As always, necessity was the mother of this invention. Aram was in financial trouble. He needed to move a little more of his noodle stock than he had been able to because the Austrian Emperor Leopold did not want non-documented "ethnics" competing with his own chefs and bakers.

Aram got around this inventory problem by baking the first noodle kugle and calling it "The Emperor Leopold Cacheznya Kugle" which everyone then knew was an enormous compliment to the Emperor even though no one knew what was being celebrated. For some reason history has forgotten the meaning of "Cacheznya." Out of this stroke of brilliant merchandising, Aram Delicatesse managed to get a dispensation and got his noodles moving. The Emperor Leopold got his name on the world's very first kugle and was pleased as punch.

The kugle went through a metamorphosis, first about 1923 in the lower eastside of New York, on Delancey Street, which raised the cholesterol count, then in the westside of Chicago which raised the sulfite content, and finally in the west—a place known as La-La Land, which lowered everything and made the noodle kugle something "modern" and wonderful!

***

INGREDIENTS, Serves 6 – 8

8 - 10 ounces	**Wide Noodles**
4 whole	**Eggs**
1 1/2 cups	**Sugar**
1/2 cup	**Pineapple,** chopped
2 cups	**Whole Milk**
1 cup	**Half and Half**
1 tablespoon	**Vanilla**
1 tablespoon	**Salt**
2 ounces	**Butter or Margarine,** melted (about 1/4 quarter cup)
1 cup	**Rasins**

METHOD

- Add noodles to boiling salted water and cook until al dente (about 1 minute).
- Drain the noodles and set aside.
- In a mixing bowl add the eggs and sugar, mix well.
- Add the raisins, pineapple, milk, half and half, butter, vanilla and noodles.

Mish mash together (Mix!). Pour into a 8 by 10 inch buttered baking dish.

- Bake at 350° for about 45 minutes. Remove and let cool.

Macaroni and Cheese

*T*he origins of this dish came from an obscure family farm on the south side of pre-Civil War Toledo, Ohio. A certain Mrs. John Burkette who had nine kids, all boys, had to use up the extra butter fat she got from the family cow.

She got her recipe down so perfectly and could do it so quickly that she and the kids ate it nearly every meal. If you're from the Midwest, anywhere near Toledo or Indianapolis, you might have an imitation recipe that pretends to be first rate. Give up.

It's a dish that one associates with an Irish home on Friday night, or with an ethnic family picnic. This is cream and butter; smooth as yogurt. It is a great American dish that has come into its own, one which has been adopted and amended to taste by the great deli cooks of our era.

How can macaroni and cheese be special? Tell me how one steak can be better than another? How can one plate of ham and eggs be better than another? How can one love affair be better than another? Trust me, it can!

We have found a prize winning macaroni and cheese formula, the creation of an executive chef for a famous Los Angeles Deli.

Don't overdo it. Remember, doors keep getting smaller.

INGREDIENTS, Serves 6 – 8

2 cups	**Elbow Macaroni**
8 cups	**Boiling Water**
2 teaspoons	**Salt** (for cooking macaroni)
2 cups	**Aged Cheddar Cheese**, grated
1 teaspoon	**Dry Mustard**
1/4 teaspoon	**Salt**
dash	**Pepper**
1 1/4 cups	**Milk**, scalded

METHOD

■ Cook the macaroni in boiling salted water for 15 minutes. Drain and rinse in hot water.

■ Place in layers in buttered baking dish sprinkling each layer with cheese, mustard, salt and pepper. Pour milk around edge and bake in a moderate oven at 350°F for 30 minutes.

■ Buttered bread crumbs or paprika may be sprinkled on top.

Cheese Blintzes

*W*ho makes cheese blintzes anymore? Someone comes over for a special breakfast and you get a few fancy sausages and scramble some eggs and buy a dozen fat bagels, pumpernickel and poppy seed and such 'cause it's just not **with it** to order plain water or egg bagels—they have to be dark or very smelly to be **with it**—and maybe you get some smoked salmon, lox to you. If it's the boss and his sweetie coming over, you buy the Nova Scotia belly lox and if just a good friend, you send him or her out to buy the lox (that's what friends are for) and are satisfied with whatever pieces or ends he or she brings back.

You can buy blintzes in the frozen food section of the super market. Who needs this recipe?

Everything I just told you is what you do if you have no class.

If you have class, you make your own blintzes. Homemade blintzes with berries and sour cream—that's class.

You go through this recipe and you're a class person; you serve this to the boss and the company's latest downsizing—the bottom line, you know—won't affect you, except you may get a promotion. You could end up being Executive Vice-President. All because of this recipe.

What does this all mean? It means that these cheese blintzes affect corporate mergers, acquisitions, downsizing and plant closings on the positive side of the ledger.

Trust me.

■ ■ ■ ■ ■ ■ ■ ■ ■

INGREDIENTS, Serves 6 – 8

2 pounds	**Hoop Cheese**
5	**Eggs**
2 tablespoons	**Sugar**
1 teaspoon	**Salt**
1 1/2 cups	**Whole Milk**
1 tablespoon	**Butter or Margarine,** melted
1 1/4 cups	**All Purpose Flour**

METHOD
Hoop Cheese Filling:
■   Mix together 2 eggs, hoop cheese, 1 tablespoon sugar and 1/2 teaspoon salt in a large bowl until well blended.

■   Cover this filling with plastic wrap and chill while you create the wrapping.

Batter & Crêpes:
■   In another large bowl using an electric mixer, blend remaining eggs, milk, melted butter, flour and the remaining sugar and salt.

■   Put mixture through a strainer to remove lumps.

■ Melt some additional butter in a crêpe pan (or 8 inch skillet) and spread on the bottom. When butter bubbles, pour in enough egg batter for a thin layer on the bottom of the pan, rotating the pan to spread the batter. Use your famous quick wrist.

■ Cook on one side until edges brown. Turn onto a paper towel and then transfer to a platter.

■ Repeat for each new crêpe and stack with wax paper between each crêpe.

■ Cover and refrigerate for ten minutes.

Assembling the Blintzes:

■ With the browned side of crêpe up, place 2 tablespoons of cheese filling on each crêpe. Fold. Tuck and make pretty.

■ Melt a tablespoon of butter in a large skillet, when it bubbles, brown each blintz **lightly**.

■ Serve with sour cream, applesauce, marinara sauce, blueberry jam, or whatever suits your taste. If you're serving the boss toss a few sprigs of Italian parsley over the dish. He'll think its very continental.

Pot Cheese and Wide Noodles

Stella Delmonica first introduced Pot Cheese and Wide Noodles to the world by serving it in her Italian delicatessen in the early fall of 1925 to please a Sicilian rum runner, Guiseppe Stephano Razia, whose mother used to make it for him when he was just a tiny little rum runner. Stella's Deli was located on Mott Street in Little Italy right near where Legs Diamond was shot down while trying to leg it out of town.

Dear Mother Razia was the one who invented the tossing of chopped chives into the recipes—and there was no way for Stella to chance upsetting a Sicilian Momma's kid.

Guiseppe came into the Deli on Wednesday and Saturday nights with his whole "gang" which he insisted Stella refer to as his "entourage"—he went to college for a year and actually knew Dorothy Parker. Business was great for Stella. She saved her money.

One Saturday night, vey iz mir, another rum runner of dubious heritage came into the Deli and, how shall I put it (?) . . . did away with Guiseppe Stephano Razia and his entire entourage. Boom, boom, bang, that's all she wrote. Stella closed up, heartbroken. The only thing she kept out of respect for and in memory of the Sicilian and the good old days was this Pot Cheese and Wide Noodles recipe.

These recipes have history, heart, love and tragedy attached to them. That's why they're so good. Maybe you serve a nice mushroom soup with this recipe. Not much else.

INGREDIENTS,   Serves 4 – 6

1 pound	**Wide Egg Noodles**
1 1/2 cups	**Pot Cheese**
1/2 teaspoon	**Butter** (or margarine)
1 teaspoon	**Salt**
1/2 teaspoon	**Rum**
1/4 cup	**Skim Milk**
1/4 cup	**Chives,** finely chopped
1/4 teaspoon	**Ground Black Pepper**

METHOD

▪ Cook noodles until done. Follow instructions on package. Don't over-cook.

▪ Drain well and pour cold water over, pat dry.

▪ Place noodles in medium pot, add cheese, butter or margarine, salt and rum.

▪ Place over a very low flame and mix in skim milk. Simmer for no more than a couple of minutes.

▪ Toss in chives, mix and serve in bowl while hot.

Pass the ground pepper at the table.

This is good the next day when heated in a Microwave, adding a touch of skim milk or water to prevent dehydrating. The touch of rum was added in memory of Guiseppe.

Kreplach

George Deets, suffering from an involuntary pre-frontal lobotomy, had been, in his glorious past, a famous French chef. He had a little black moustache and a funny twitch he was always fighting. Just a little tic that made his head jerk a little and his Bing Crosby ears flap now and then. He would often sit alone in his wicker chair contemplating the world.

What happened to poor George was that he was once asked to cater the wedding of a local (Des Moines, Iowa) Jewish Cantor to a Shinto High Priestess. They had met one another on a Kasha Kibbutz near Mobile, Alabama. This story is absolutely true—check with the Mobile, Alabama Triple A.

While steaming a mackerel to be served with chives and a sour cream sauce, he was asked by the bride's Momma, Passover Priscilla, to prepare six dozen Kreplach for the Creme Boule soup he was creating. He was given the recipe by Passover Priscilla.

George tried very hard to please. Really hard. But try as he might he succeeded in producing only small leaden flatware disks solely suitable for bombarding rabid Texans who persistently attacked over the border trying to make amends for the Alamo defeat a hundred years earlier.

George went downhill fast. It didn't take long.

He stood over his stove repeatedly muttering terrible things about Passover Priscilla as each Kreplach came out. He started screaming, too. Incomprehensible things which everyone was glad were incomprehensible. Nothing seemed to bring him out of it. Needless to say the wedding did not go well. George was eventually dragged away from the stove blubbering weird things like, "My Kingdom for a Horse!" which no one understood. So they eased his pain by operating, which, as you know, is what doctors do when they're perplexed. They generously provided George with a pre-frontal lobotomy and a horse and the luxury of never having to see Passover Priscilla or hear her name again.

The Priestess and the Cantor are still married. She cooks kreplach and he cooks matzo balls from the recipes in this book. They visit poor George Deets regularly.

This sad story could have been avoided with the following recipe. Think of it as a soul saving one.

INGREDIENTS, Serves 6 - 8

      Dough for Kreplach:

2 cups	**Flour**
1/2 cup	**Salad Oil**
4 whole	**Eggs**

      Meat Filling:

2 pounds	**Ground Chuck**
1 1/2 pounds	**Onions,** diced small
1 tablespoon	**Salt**
1 teaspoon	**Ground Black Pepper**

METHOD For Dough:

- In a large bowl mish mash all the kreplach ingredients together well.
- Form into a ball and set aside.

METHOD For Meat Filling:

- In another bowl mix the ground chuck, onions, salt and pepper.
- Roll the dough out creating 4 inch squares of thin dough.
Place about an ounce of meat mixture in each square.
- Place another square of dough on top. Moisten edges with
water and pinch ends together.
- Cook in boiling salted water for about 15 minutes.

This kreplach recipe can substitute for a Chinese dumpling or an Italian ravioli depending on what you fill it with. You can even deep fry the result instead of boiling, add plum sauce on the side and Voilá!—a deep fried Chinese appetizer, $4.95.

Quick Bricked Chicken Breast

*T*he **First Mother** *was also the* **First Mother-In-Law**. *She* **had** *to be because she was the only one. I remember distinctly her saying to me; "Adam is good with greens. And chicken breasts, too. But don't show him those damn red apples."*

Everyone's troubles stem from the fact that someone just refused to listen. We know what happened. Along came kids who wanted whatever they saw and who refused to wear clothes which were required after the red apple incident. They kept saying things like—"But this is the 60's!" which I didn't understand unless they meant 6060 BC. Then came all the problems . . . Issac mixing it up with God about his kid, Commandments coming down from The Mountain, grandchildren wandering around in the desert for 40 years, normal everyday stuff; high school proms, acne, loud neighbors, silly in-laws, bill collectors.

Some residents up in heaven, where all the good Deli cooks reside, insist you must stay away from red apples offered by big snakes and from cooks who tinker with Breasts.

I really don't agree. What do they know?

INGREDIENTS, Serves 4 – 5

1 clean	**Brick**
3 pounds	**Frying Chicken,** butterflied or without backbone removed
1/2 cup	**Fresh Lemon Juice**
1/4 cup	**Virgin Olive Oil**
1 clove	**Garlic,** minced (or 1/2 teaspoon bottled minced garlic)
1 sprig	**Fresh Rosemary,** minced
1 teaspoon	**Parsley,** minced
1/2 teaspoon	**Salt** (or to taste)
1/2 teaspoon	**Crushed Pepper**

METHOD

- Soak the brick in hot water.
- Remove wings from chicken—open and press flat.
- Mix all condiments in a large shallow pyrex dish.
- Place butterflied chicken and separate wings in the dish—make sure all parts of chicken get a dose of marinade and soak for 2 – 3 hours.
- Preheat large skillet until good and hot.
- Add about 2 tablespoons olive oil to skillet.
- Place chicken on hot skillet.
- Place soaked brick on top.
- Brown over high heat about 5 minutes each side or until crisp.
- Option—peel and slice skin away—replace into skillet 1/2 minute each side.

- Or serve with crispy skin while hot.
- Save brick for unwanted intruders.

This is a quick fried chicken recipe that results in a golden brown and succulent fried chicken. Best served with Caesar salad, hot green beans.

Chopped Liver

Before the modern era every kid had to eat liver once a week. It began somewhere around the 5th Century—BC! How to get kids to eat what they hate?? After all, kids are smarter than the rest of us, especially between the ages of fourteen and nineteen.

Mama figured it out. Chop it, fix it, smooth it out, make it spread on cookies and crackers; in short, disguise it by making it wonderful. When you need a quick fix of "down home" no one does it quite as well as a really hot shot local Delicatessen. And, with a good chopped liver at your local deli, you also get valet parking, a wise-cracking waitress, a maitre D' who mispronounces your name into a cheap PA system, and rye bread.

There's a tiny Deli a stone's throw from the Vatican, right off one of the side-streets. When the Pope secretly succumbs to his need for a fix of chopped liver he sends out for their dinner portion, eats half and hides the rest until an appropriate midnight.

This is the recipe they use.

INGREDIENTS, Serves 8 – 10

2 pounds	**Baby Beef Liver,** diced
3 pounds	**Onions,** diced
3 pounds	**Bread Crumbs**
4	**Eggs**
4 ounces	**Salad Oil or Chicken Fat**
3 teaspoons	**Salt**
1 teaspoon	**Black Pepper**

METHOD

■ Cook the liver in boiling water for about 30 to 45 minutes or until well done.

■ Remove the liver and cool by running cold water over it. Drain and set aside.

■ Saute the onions in the oil or chicken fat until lightly browned. Remove from the heat and let cool.

■ Place the eggs in a pot of boiling water and cook for 10 minutes. Remove the eggs and put under running cold water to cool. Peel the eggs and set aside.

■ In a mixing bowl, add the liver, onions with oil, bread crumbs, hard boiled eggs, salt and pepper. Mix well and put through a medium food grinder. Refrigerate.

This recipe will keep 3 – 4 days if covered and refrigerated. Great afternoon snack with crackers and apple-cinnamon hot tea and good company.

Salads

Avocado Salad–Deli Style

I have an ancient very Catholic aunt—Aunt Margaret. She is eighty-nine and doing well, thank you. She has always lived in the same house, a two-story California style bungalow that was once part of an immense orchard of navel and valencia oranges which has disappeared into the abyss of time. The house was built in 1912. Shortly after that Margie's father planted an avocado tree in its back yard. That tree still flourishes. It is a great tree, a monumental tree, more than four stories tall and as wide as the Queen Mary amidship. It falls over the ochre hued house in great green branches that possess a sheen reflecting shafts of green and yellow light in differing shades at different times of the day. Its branches hang untrimmed down into the yard, falling every which way over the property, held up here and there by thick wooden supports, creating a soft ground cover of leafy mulch that becomes its own compost so that it flourishes even more. It grows enormous numbers of fruit, perfect fruit. You can't reach or pick all the hundreds of avocados hanging from its branches.

Aunt Margie will not permit anyone to trim the tree. No one is allowed to touch even a leaf, or to prevent a branch from falling into a pathway or onto another tree. It is as though that tree is an extension of Margie. It is she! A gorgeous, stately living thing that will endure another hundred years; a real and true part of her and her belief in life, in the sacred state of living, of enduring now and beyond her years in her own inimitable way.

Each one of us has something that is part of us that we do not want touched, altered, played with or dismantled. Now and then these castles which are to remain untouched are not good for us; they deceive us, do us no service, but we guard them zealously.

I can understand Aunt Margaret's obsession.

Like her view of the great avocado tree, the following cannot be altered, played with, trimmed, or hurried through.

INGREDIENTS, Serves 6

1 large	**Avocado,** peeled, seeded and sliced in decorative slices
2 cups	**Butter Lettuce or Red Leaf Lettuce,** chopped
1 cup	**Watercress,** chopped
1/2 cup	**Black Olives,** pitted
1/2 cup	**Porcini Mushrooms,** sliced
1/2 cup	**Garlic Croutons**
2	**Hard Boiled Eggs,** chopped
2 large slices	**Swiss Cheese,** julienne sliced (about 1/2 cup)
as needed	**Vinaigrette Dressing**

Vinaigrette Dressing:

1/4 cup	**Olive Oil (mild)**
1/4 cup	**Red Wine Vinegar**
1 tablespoon	**Capers,** drained
1/2 teaspoon	**Minced Garlic**
1/2 teaspoon	**Dijon Mustard** (or mustard of your preference)
1/4 teaspoon	**Salt**
1/4 teaspoon	**Black Pepper,** ground

METHOD–SALAD

■ Slice avocado in half and remove seed.

■ Slice thin slices from each half of avocado for decorative effect.

■ Toss everything except avocado, swiss cheese and the dressing into large salad bowl and toss.

■ Place cheese slices and avocado slices on top in decorative fashion.

■ Shake the vinaigrette dressing and pour about half of it over the salad. Place the remaining dressing in a small serving dish with spoon.

METHOD–SALAD DRESSING

■ Combine all ingredients of the vinaigrette in a jar with cap and mix.

■ Chill 1/2 hour.

■ Shake well before using.

The garlic in this gives it the zest the avocado deserves. You can add a touch of garlic powder if your taste is up to it.

Chinese Chicken Salad

*N*o one from the upper reaches of the Yangtze River ever heard of Chinese Chicken Salad. It doesn't exist in reality—only in the mind's eye. One **sees and feels** something "Chinese" in a salad that sports a handful of dried **noodles**. It's a distortion of reality.

Once, in a Chicago public library, I saw a brittle little lady, great big darting green eyes, indoor skin, a tiny nose, searching intently through a very thick book about twice her size. She had a set of spectacles hanging from a yellow string onto her bosom. Suddenly she grunted "Aha!" And swept her spectacles onto the tip of her tiny nose and through the gold rims poked that little nose and wide eyes deeper into her enormous book. Only then did I notice that there were no lenses within the rims of her glasses. Only air. Whatever she was seeking was restricted to her mind's eye; the same one that distorts reality when we see, feel or taste something Chinese in a salad, or something sexy about a fresh open oyster.

What great things we wring out of our mind's eye! A look, a texture, a taste that we persuade ourselves is Chinese. Our recipe arises from your willingness to bend reality into a moment of culinary joy. It's all quite wonderful, isn't it?

■ ■ ■ ■ ■

INGREDIENTS, Serves 8
   Dressing:

1/2 cup	**Red Wine Vinegar**
2 tablespoons	**Light Soy Sauce**
2 tablespoons	**Sesame Oil**
1/4 cup	**Syrup from a jar of preserved Ginger in syrup** (find in ethnic sections of grocery store)
1 tablespoon	**Hoisin Sauce**
to taste	**Salt**
to taste	**Ground Pepper**
1/2 cup	**Green Onions,** minced
Smidgen	**Chili Powder**
Salad:	
2	**Chicken Breasts,** cooked, skinned and shredded
4 cups	**Romaine Lettuce,** Shredded (about 2 heads)
1 1/2 cups	**Bean Sprouts**
1	**Red Bell Pepper,** diced
1/2 cup	**Almonds,** shredded or slivered
10 – 12	**Wonton Skins**
2 cups	**Peanut Oil,** for frying
2 ounces	**Rice Sticks**
1/2 cup	**Ginger (preserved in syrup),** thinly sliced

METHOD

■ Combine all salad dressing ingredients into medium bowl and blend well. Cover and chill.

■ In a large bowl combine the chicken, lettuce, bean sprouts and bell pepper. Cover and refrigerate.

■ Place almonds on aluminum foil and place into a 325 – 350° oven until golden (about 15 – 18 minutes).

■ Heat oil in a 12 inch skillet.

■ Slice wontons into quarter inch strips.

■ Test the heat of the oil by dropping a wonton strip into it, when it dances on the surface add the wontons and fry them until they are golden brown. Remove and drain on a paper towel.

■ Fry rice sticks in the oil (be sure it is very hot). They will quickly expand. Turn them over (**don't use your fingers**) and cook a few more seconds. Remove and drain. Let them cool (can be prepared a few hours ahead).

■ Mix into the salad mixture the almonds, ginger, chicken and vegetables. Toss very gently.

■ Add to the salad mixture the wonton skins and the rice sticks, gently mix.

■ Shake the salad dressing and add to the salad, tossing gently. Serve within a quarter of an hour.

The only way this could be more Chinese is if you added pigtails which I instruct you not to do.

Celery Root Salad

*C*elery root is one of those ugly things you see in the vegetable bins that you would never buy because the silly thing just doesn't look edible, or clean, or cheap enough to try. This is how it got legitimate.

Elianahuu Rootless, son of Rolph Rootless II, the famous seventeenth century horticulturist from whom all roots are named, insisted that his most wonderful root creation was fashioned out of that big dirty celery "thing."

Unknown to the populace at large, his mother's father was half Jewish—he wasn't certain which half—and his mother's father's cousin was a devout and practicing Jewish grandmother. Resulting from this secret past was his penchant for hovering over everyone's shoulder as they ate, celery root in hand, pleading for people to try it . . . "Just try it. It couldn't hurt"—which is how the root got its name. "Celery" is the Celtic-Armenian derivation of the phrase—"it couldn't hurt."

Finally the local Baroness of the High Holy Spirit of Hot Cross Buns grabbed the root from Rootless's hands, cut it in half, ate a bite and immediately started to make love to the man next to her who happened to be a waiter with an open button near an appealing nipple. Well, the waiter was instantly beheaded and the Baroness was leased out to a number of other Barons because of the sensation she made after taking a bite of that celery root.

It is said, in whispers, that even the waiter died content. It is also said, in whispers, that this Celery Root Salad has caused severe marital discord in some families . . . but you should ignore such whispers, be brave—give it a try.

■ ■ ■ ■ ■

INGREDIENTS, Serves 4

3 tablespoons	**Light Mayonnaise**
2 tablespoons	**Dijon Mustard**—(more?)
1 teaspoon	**Garlic, minced**
3/4 teaspoon	**White Wine Vinegar**
1 1/2 pounds	**Celery Root,** grated
1/4 cup	**Fresh Parsley,** chopped
1/2 teaspoon	**Salt**
1/2 teaspoon	**Ground Pepper**

METHOD

■ Bring a quart of water to a boil, meanwhile:

■ Mix together the mayonnaise, Dijon mustard, vinegar and minced garlic—taste for the hell of it. The amount of mustard and mayo varies with taste.

■ Peel the celery root and grate it into thin slices about 1 to 2 inches long.

■ Place the slices of celery root in a large bowl with cold water and toss in the salt and pepper. Let stand 15 minutes.

■ Transfer to colander and pour the boiling water over it, then rinse with cold water.

■ In a large bowl toss the celery root with the sauce and a tablespoon of the parsley. Sprinkle the remaining parsley over the top—do not mix in.

■ Add another touch of vinegar if too dry for your taste.

■ Chill and serve (using an ice cream scooper) on a leaf or two of red lettuce or butter lettuce.

This is the world's greatest starter for a summer dinner. Pungent, lively, different.

Potato Salad

Mark Twain once worried that potatoes might restrain passion. Indeed, he had a lengthy correspondence with the most famous journalist of his day, Horace Greeley, on the subject of whether potatoes or turnips were the culprits.

After experimentation, Twain decided that Greeley was the quintessential neurotic and that potatoes had positive effects on one's libido, particularly **his** *libido. Twain avoided turnips for the rest of his life. I do the same.*

In fact, as a result of Mark Twain's experimentation, many men refused to eat potatoes when on lonely, male orientated explorations of the wild west where women were few, far between and uncertain objects of potato driven passion.

In this modern complex era of planes, tanks, lawyers and psychiatrists, it has been known that wives now and then complain about the libidos of their mates. We can urge upon all persons—potatoes—particularly potato salad, which is the final formula in the preparation and presentation of this passionate vegetable.

The following recipe is the best of the best of the varied potato salad recipes.

■ ■ ■ ■ ■ ■

INGREDIENTS, Serves 4

Salad:

1 pound	**Small Red Potatoes,** peeled and cubed
1 Small	**Sweet Red Pepper,** cored and diced
1/2 cup	**Celery,** diced
3	**Shallots,** chopped fine
1/4 cup	**Chives,** chopped

Dressing:

1 tablespoon	**Lemon Juice**
1 tablespoon	**Tarragon Vinegar**
1 1/2 teaspoon	**Dijon Mustard** (more?)
1 clove	**Garlic,** minced (or a full teaspoon bottled minced garlic)
1/4 teaspoon	**Salt** (or to taste)
1/4 teaspoon	**Ground Pepper** (or to taste)
1/4 cup	**Chicken Stock or Broth**
1 tablespoon	**Olive Oil**
3 tablespoons	**Various Minced Herbs** (basil, chervil, tarragon, etc.)
2 tablespoons	**Sour Cream**
1 teaspoon	**Mayonnaise** (low fat)
1/2 teaspoon	**White Horseradish** (optional)
1/2 teaspoon	**Dill Weed**

METHOD

■ Place potatoes in a steamer basket, set in boiling water 10 minutes, until tender, not mushy.

■ Place drained potatoes in a large bowl, add peppers, celery, shallots and chives.

■ In a separate bowl whisk together all the dressing ingredients, one at a time. Whisk until well blended (or place into a jar and shake).

■ Pour into a large bowl and toss. Chill until ready to serve.

You don't need to wait for heaven, merely serve this with half a salami on rye sandwich and a black cherry soda.

Macaroni Salad

You think you've heard this old cooking story before, but you haven't. Fred Himmelfarb insists on having the grandest Bar Mitzvah known to mankind for his boy child, Silas Himmelfarb. It was to be a Bar Mitzvah never to be equalled in a place never before seen. The kid has freckles and is a little dull, but no matter. Fred hires the Barnum and Bailey's Circus—the entire circus, the Crown Prince Khaled of Ethiopia and his princely entourage as guides to the unknown parts of deepest Africa—Stanley and Livingston both couldn't find their way; and —wait—he lands Wolfgang Puck to cater the affair!

He invites six hundred guests, an extra fifty-six elephants, and off they go to a tiny spot on the map believed never to have seen black men, white men, Irishmen, never a woman, and certainly not a Bar Mitzvah catered affair.

They crash through the jungle for days, the Ethiopian Prince keeps pressing on. Fred Himmelfarb keeps everyone's spirits up with performances of the circus acrobats and by dancing the Khaszatska every night in front of the massive campfire. They are getting close. They have to be getting close because Prince Khaled says "soon." They send scouts on ahead. One day the scouts come back shouting, "Up ahead! up ahead!—Oh, my God!" What? What? "We're going back to check again!" What?

In an hour they come back in a state of intense shock. The Ethiopians are as pale as sheet rock so you can imagine their condition. "A thousand Zulus and seventeen nasty waitresses in a clearing, all mumbling tribal incantations, baking apple croissants and making macaroni salad!!"

How could that be? "Oh my God" is right. Fred gets his report—"Abe Schneiderman and his Bar Mitzvah boy got here three months ago and opened a huge Delicatessen!—with leather booths and take out! The Zulus do the cooking . . . seventeen nasty waitresses all of whom chew gum . . . they say they've been holding a reservation for us!"

Which only goes to prove that you can't even guess at what you don't know. Ain't it the truth?

INGREDIENTS,   Serves 7 – 8

1/4 cup	**Light Mayonnaise**
4 tablespoons	**Dijon Mustard**
2 tablespoons	**Lemon Juice**
dash	**Wine Vinegar**
1	**Shallot,** minced
1/4 cup	**Fresh Chives,** chopped
dash	**Salt**
1/2 teaspoon	**Ground Pepper**
8 – 10 ounces	**Elbow Macaroni**
1 cup	**Celery,** diced

¹/4 cup	**Fennel Bulb,** diced
¹/2 cup	**Red and Green Bell Peppers,** diced
¹/4 cup	**Green Onions,** diced
¹/4 cup	**Fresh Parsley,** chopped

METHOD

■ In a small bowl blend together the mayonnaise, Dijon mustard, lemon juice, wine vinegar, shallots, chives, salt and a little pepper. Cover with plastic wrap and chill an hour or so, or a day or so. It will keep a while.

■ Cook elbow macaroni in boiling, salted water until al dente. Drain well.

■ In large bowl combine cooked macaroni with about ¹/2 cup of the mayonnaise-vinaigrette. Chill the macaroni mixture in the fridge for about an hour.

■ Combine the celery, fennel, bell peppers, onions and parsley with the macaroni mixture.

■ Add the remaining mayo-vinaigrette mixture, adding ground pepper to taste. Mix well.

If you serve this fresh it has a nice crunch to it. You can refrigerate this but some of the freshness of the celery and fennel will diminish. Even so, you'll love it. Great for summer evenings.

Deli Style

Soups
and
Sandwiches

Chicken Soup

"Chicken Soup" is the name of a religion. When Moses came over the mountain he looked down at Canaan, over the river Jordan, and said "Chicletsferall" which his companions took to mean "Chicken Soup."

And so it came to pass.

"Chicken Soup" took fire and spread around the globe—which only took a week or so because the globe was smaller then than now. So, there you are; Moses died, Canaan was secured, and "Chicken Soup" kept going and growing in prestige and power. Every grandmother in ancient Palestine believed in it. This was, as you know, a very powerful force.

Today "Chicken Soup" (for believers) cures a fever, a cold, the flu, undefined aches and pains, is known in every nook and cranny of the globe—which is much bigger now than then, and is the subject of more printed words than then.

Assume an appropriate reverential mind-set when attempting this recipe.

■ ■ ■ ■ ■

INGREDIENTS, Serves 4 *This recipe eliminates residue and fat content.*

1 whole	**Roasting Chicken,** cleaned and washed
1 gallon	**Water,** cold
8 ounces	**Onions,** chopped (1 cup)
8 ounces	**Celery,** chopped (1 cup)
8 ounces	**Carrots,** chopped (1 cup)
2 teaspoons	**Salt**
1/4 teaspoon	**Black Pepper** (or a pinch)

METHOD

■ Bring the whole chicken and water to a simmer. If the chicken is less than 3 pounds, cheat a little and toss in a couple of bouillon cubes—maybe toss one in anyway and don't tell.

■ Add the celery, carrots and onions. Cook for 1 1/2 hours at a slow boil .

■ Remove the chicken. Remove the skin and dispose of it. Remove the vegetables and set aside with the chicken.

■ Skim the fat from the broth and strain from one pot to another. A better way is to refrigerate the broth and remove the fat from the top the next day.

■ Chop the chicken and vegetables together and add to the broth. Season with salt and pepper. Heat **slowly** to a boil. Add noodles or rice or whatever and serve.

Matzo Balls

Matzo Balls have a history. Not a very interesting one except they were invented sometime after the Exodus. The first Exodus. Every culture has its own Matzo Balls. Dumplings, Ravioli, Egg Rolls . . . like that.

My former mother-in-law served them every Friday night. They were the size of Ping-Pong balls and about as heavy as Uranium-235. I would surreptitiously pocket them and arrange vast scenarios for their disappearance down street drains. I didn't want my wife to catch me. A natural and reasonable subterfuge. Except, it didn't work. That wife divorced me. You can't be too careful with a mother-in-law's Matzo Balls.

Some home recipes make these babies as big as softballs figuring big meant soft and fluffy. It doesn't. They ought to be about the size of a handball.

My mother once got her zeros mixed up and made over two hundred of them for a Passover Dinner for twenty celebrants. We had to get the gas company to turn off the gas in the house in order to stop her. She was persistent if nothing else. We tried to give them away but go find a Protestant who wants a hundred and fifty stale Matzo Balls!

A good Deli Matzo Ball has a touch of flavor, is not too big and not too heavy and no one uses them in place of the real thing in baseball games

INGREDIENTS, Serves 6 – 8

1 1/2 pounds	**Matzo Meal**
6	**Eggs, whole**
6 ounces	**Salad Oil** (use corn oil, olive oil is not good here)
1 tablespoon	**Salt**
1/4 teaspoon	**White Pepper**
1 tablespoon	**Baking Powder**
1	**Pot, Boiling Water**
1 ounce	**Scoop**

METHOD

■ Mix the first six ingredients well, and let rest for 15 minutes.

■ Bring the pot of water to a slow boil. Scoop out the matzo balls with a 1 ounce scoop and place them in the boiling water, let them cook until the balls rise to the top. Remove the matzo balls from the pot and place into cold water to cool. Once they are cool, remove from cold water and refrigerate.

Navy Bean Soup

*T*he USS Mother Teresa, a heavily armed nuclear United States cruiser class battleship, was steaming towards Madagascar to land a party of the **Mongolian Infiltrator Ladies Kaboom Force,** known as the **MILK FORCE**. The purpose was to capture the leaders of the **NoCookingAnymo for Males over eighteen years of Age** rebellion, known as the NMA.

Men from this island can't cook, or do most other things—except make speeches, as the women of the rebellion knew. These men are very famous for speechifying and they are sometimes surreptitiously imported into the U.S. House of Representatives as midnight-empty-house stand-ins for slow-witted Congressmen. The respective chiefs of the political parties figured importing these lazy sonofabitches was better than letting some of the elected dopes loose on the House of Representatives even though it was midnight and the place was empty.

As you can imagine, the island's democratic processes were faltering; men were starving because women of the rebellion weren't cooking or sewing or . . . you know.

On the way, near a boulevard stop in the Indian Ocean, the clatzratchet of the USS Mother Teresa stopped working. All the sailors ran around in circles trying to fix it, although they took a day off for the Tailhook Affair. Finally, the Captain called their insurance company as per his secret instructions, but the insurance company said that the Mother Teresa was only covered while steaming in the Atlantic Ocean on Thursdays, between eight and nine a.m., north of the equator and by the way, your insurance is cancelled because you filed a claim last year involving more than thirty-five dollars. The insurance adjuster, however, being always helpful as most adjusters are, suggested that sometimes navy bean soup works in clatzratchet situations.

Mylanta be damned, the Captain poured his best 100 gallon batch of navy bean soup into the nuclear tank (or whatever) and the Mother Teresa took off like a shot.

The MILK FORCE landed and captured the leaders of NMA and the remaining women *began to cook again. This was, of course, a failure of USA foreign policy which has since been corrected by political pressure from NOW.*

The following recipe is the only one in the entire world that will not propel a USS cruiser class navy battleship

INGREDIENTS, Serves 6 – 8

2 cups	**Navy Beans**
I cup	**Celery,** diced
I cup	**White Onions,** diced
I cup	**Carrots,** diced
I teaspoon	**Black Pepper**
2	**Bay Leaves**
3 6 oz. cans	**Chicken Broth, low fat**
$^1/_2$ teaspoon	**Salt**

METHOD

■ Soak beans in luke-warm water for at least two hours.

■ Drain.

■ Pour into large cooking pot.

■ Add the vegetables and seasonings and 2 cups of chicken broth.

■ Cook for at least an hour on low to medium flame, adding more chicken broth about every 10 minutes as needed.

Beet Borscht

*I*n 1841, August I think it was, anyway it was a Tuesday in the middle of the year, the grandfather of the famous Russian actor, Mischa Auer, who was also named Mischa, jumped his Russian ship in the Bering sea and with the help of Aluit Eskimos eventually got to Seattle, which a substantial number of you know is in the state of Washington.

Mischa carried with him a bottle of beets and beet juice which he affection-ately called BJ and from which he wanted to make Vodka or a dye for a new Russian Flag. He didn't succeed in getting the blend he wanted for either purpose and since he was persistently drunk on BJ wine he was unperturbed with his failures. Indeed, he seemed quite happy to fail and drink, fail and drink and fail and drink.

One day while in his mugs he dropped a scoop of Russian Sour Cream into one of his reddish vodkabeet concoctions and gave it to his then mistress, Leanna Podgorthy Vladivostoc Sikorskian, a Russian-Armenian-Mongolian slightly zaftig beauty from Khazachstan. She took a drink, insisted that Mischa try a drink, whereupon he immediately began dancing a Khazatscka and forthwith instituted the development of the concoction into a soup he called **Biscaposka** which in Mongolian means, **"whatever."**

Bit by bit he got this recipe into shape.

Leanna didn't like the name—**Biscaposka**. Who would buy Biscaposka in Orlando? Or Mobile? Or Colorado Junction? You couldn't sell it to the Indians because they couldn't pronounce it.

Leanna Podgorthy worked on the name while Mischa worked on the recipe.

Finally Mischa came up with his Beet and Sour Cream Soup. However, he was dying for a Vodka. So he shoved his Beet Soup aside, fermented an old potato and went back to his old ways, fail and drink, fail and drink.

Leanna Podgorthy Vladivostoc Sikorskian took the old Beet Soup formula to a local Delicatessen and you know the rest.

The lesson in life herein is that a person shouldn't jump ship in the middle of the Bering Sea without a very good plan.

INGREDIENTS, Serves 4 or more

2 bunches	**Beets,** unpeeled
12 cups	**Water**
3/4 cup	**Sugar**
2 1/2 teaspoons	**Salt**
1/2 cup	**Lemon Juice**
to taste	**Sour Cream**

METHOD

- Cut off top—scrub beets clean.
- Boil beets in water until barely tender, 5 – 10 minutes.
- Remove beets and place into a large bowl and peel. Save water.
- Grate beets into thin 1/2 inch to 1 inch pieces.
- Return grated beets to water and add water to bring up to 12 cups. Add sugar, salt and lemon juice. Boil 15 minutes.
- Add additional sugar or salt to taste.
- Refrigerate 2 or more hours.
- Serve with sour cream in tablespoon heaps.

Toss a clove or two in pot to add a little zest to flavor. Borscht and Macaroni salad is what Polish Kings demanded for royal feasts. They have disappeared, as you may have noticed, but, really, were they wrong?

Cabbage Soup

*T*here is a largely ignored Criminal Code against Cookery Crimes. You know the criminals—most of them habitual. We ought to throw away the key. The latest crimes and the penalties are prescribed by the Code of Cookery Crimes, Volume 3; Section 2(b):

1. The cook who warms french fries in the microwave = one year county jail and a minimum fine of $500.

2. Pan frying a steak with a weight on top = two years in Alcatraz reopened especially for you.

3. Failing to re-rinse spinach leaves = six months suspended sentence plus community service and spinach with every meal.

4. Finishing the vegetables for your dinner party a half hour before the entree is done = six months to be served as fry cook for Georgie Baby's Cajun Curlers restaurant just outside Tucumcari, New Mexico.

5. Large beautiful and tall centerpiece on the dining room table during dinner = one year county jail time and minimum $500 fine.

6. Displaying your ecumenical nature by serving Afganistanian food to twenty visiting Russian dignitaries = 10 years San Quentin.

7. Dinner prayer in Latin = 6 months or $250 fine or both.

8. Dinner prayers for Buddhist neighbors with repeated signs of the cross = one year, no time off for good behavior.

9. Burnt toast on Sunday mornings = 18 hours of The Silent Treatment which is nearly as bad as Alcatraz at night.

10. Too much salt and/or too little garlic = death.

No mistakes. No Cookery Crimes.

INGREDIENTS, Serves 6 – 8

1 cup	**Tomato Puree**
1 cup	**Tomato Juice**
1/2 cup	**Lemon Juice**
1 cup	**Water**
4 cups	**Cabbage,** shredded
2 small	**Cloves**
2 small	**Black Peppercorns,** whole
3 tablespoons	**Salt**

METHOD

■ Toss all ingredients except salt into a large pot. Bring to a boil and reduce heat to a simmer, skimming the surface if necessary.

■ After half hour add salt and simmer another 15 – 20 minutes. The cabbage should be tender but not limp.

Mushroom Barley Soup

*Y*ou can't use those funny mushrooms for a deli soup. It wouldn't do to get arrested while you're creating a soup, so you have to use the particular mushrooms recommended herein and none of the funny stuff.

I know someone's momma who thinks the mushroom barley soup always comes out too thick and wants it thinned with broth. She complains to the waitress and when it comes back she complains again that it's too thin. It never fails. Then this person's mother asks for a new bowl—with the same result—and then the manager comes over and asks her to leave. The ritual has been given a name—The Deli Dance.

It's the combination of ingredients, the type of mushroom, the nature of the veggies, that make this recipe special in a good deli, not too thick and not too thin, and not so special anywhere else. A good Mushroom/Barley soup is the epitome of Delicatessen cuisine. In spite of that someone's momma.

INGREDIENTS, Serves 8 – 10

10 cups	**Water**
1 cup	**Pearl Barley**
3/4 cup	**Carrots**, diced
3/4 cup	**Onions**, chopped
1/2 cup	**Celery**, diced
1 cup	**Chicken Bouillon**
1 teaspoon	**Salt**
1/2 teaspoon	**White Pepper**
1/2 cup	**Dried Mushrooms** (porcini or shiitake)

METHOD

- Soak the dried mushrooms in cold water for 15 minutes.
- Mix all ingredients in a soup pot. Bring to a boil for 5 minutes. Reduce the heat and cook for 2 1/2 hours.

Monte Cristo

*T*he Count of Monte Cristo was like the Batman of his day—no one could touch him. He could take his sword and cut a candle in half and leave it standing; leap from precipice to precipice and not even stub a toe; demolish all the bad guys with one mighty stroke of his really sharp rapier. The Joker didn't stand a chance. I mean The Count was one of a kind.

Even Batman didn't get 400 pages—no pictures— in a hard cover best seller. The Count of Monte Cristo didn't have a disguise either. No black hood or big red S's on his chest. You never knew when the Count was around. He might be your neighbor living in that castle just down the road. Kids were on their good behavior and ate their vegetables just thinking about the Count of Monte Cristo.

Is it any wonder, then, that the King's Royal Cooks created this knife and fork deep fried sandwich just to please the Count? It was and is one of a kind.

Serve this and who knows who will come crashing down from the chandeliers, flashing sword in hand, to save you from the burnt peas and dry casserole.

INGREDIENTS, Makes 1 sandwich

2 tablespoons	**Margarine**
1/2 teaspoon	**Dijon Mustard**
3 slices	**White or Wheat Bread**
3 slices	**Turkey**
1 slice	**Mozzarella Cheese**
3 slices	**Baked Ham,** not too thick
1/4 cup each	**Vegetable and Olive Oil**
2	**Eggs**
Smidgen	**Milk**
Smidgen	**Salt and Pepper**

METHOD

■ In a small bowl blend the margarine and mustard, spread on all sides of bread.

■ Assemble the sandwiches, placing the turkey and cheese on one slice of bread, top with a second slice of bread, followed by the ham and last piece of bread.

■ Cut sandwich in half diagonally.

■ Make batter by blending eggs, milk, salt and pepper (you want to try a smidgen of garlic powder?).

■ In a deep skillet pour in the oils about 1 1/2 to 2 inches deep. Heat until good and hot (400°F).

■ Dip sandwich halves into batter and thoroughly soak. Deep fry, taking care that the sandwich is not treated roughly during the frying so that it stays together.

■ When done, stick fancy toothpicks in each half. Place thin slices of cantaloupe on the plate with a little parsley. Serve with jelly, powdered sugar, or a touch of maple syrup—to each his or her own.

Reuben Sandwich

I had a friend, Harry, who was quite ill and bed ridden. He was younger than I, yet looked a generation older. He still had a sweet smile. His large droopy blue eyes had a way of enjoying the moment whatever pain he was suffering.

He loved Reuben Sandwiches and the doctor said, "What the hell, go ahead and let him enjoy." So I brought him Reuben Sandwiches, one from this place and that place, from an eastside deli, from a westside deli, from all around town. We finally found the one he liked the best which, naturally, was a half dollar more than the others. We gave it a name—Harry's Friend. I visited once or twice a week and always brought Harry's Friend. It was a serious ritual.

One Tuesday I was in his neighborhood and went over to his place without stopping to get his Reuben Sandwich. I caught him by surprise. He was upset to the point of tears that I didn't bring Harry's Friend along. Yet last week's Reuben was sitting on his dresser, with one bite out of it. I asked him if he always ate his Reuben Sandwiches and he smiled. What a beautiful smile! His eyes widened and he said, "My friend and I understand one another. Sometimes I can eat it up and sometimes I can't but I don't want you to stop bringing him. I hide that part of him that I can't eat so you don't get upset, like today. A little here, a little there. He doesn't mind. I don't mind. We're secret sharers . . ."

Then he added, "Expectations, good friend, expectations make life worth living." Harry died soon after.

Expectations. They make life quite difficult and yet can make life quite wonderful.

This recipe was Harry's Friend.

— ■ ■ ■ ■ ■ ■ —

INGREDIENTS, Serves 2

¹/₂ pound	**Corned Beef,** sliced
4 slices	**Swiss Cheese**
³/₄ pound	**Sauerkraut**
2 large slices	**Rye Bread**
I tablespoon	**Margarine, Butter or Spray Margarine** (as needed)
I tablespoon	**Dijon Mustard**

METHOD

- Heat large skillet and add margarine, butter or spray margarine until bubbly.
- Place rye bread in pan, flip bread after several minutes, adding more margarine or butter as needed.
- Spread a little Dijon mustard on each slice, add corned beef (dividing equally on each slice of bread), sauerkraut and cheese. Add Russian dressing.
- Grill for about 2 or 3 minutes.
- Slice bread into 4 equal parts, garnish with parsley around the edges if the sandwich is for company. Serve with potato salad or coleslaw and diluted cranberry juice over ice.

This recipe can be prepared over a charcoal grill. Instead of pan frying, merely spread a thin layer of spray margarine on bread and place on the grill, following the recipe above. Try to keep the corn beef and other ingredients on the bread so as to avoid them dripping onto the fire.

voluptuous

Potato Knish

*A*n ingenious Irishman took his last potato, maybe the last left in all of
Ireland and high-tailed it out of the country. It was September, 1846.
*During the famine. He carried what had become a mushy potato onto the boat
to the USA and showed it to a Russian Jewish pastry cook from Minsk who
showed it to a displaced Lithuanian Catholic from Murmansk.*

*The three of them were interested in a business relationship in the new world
so they made a deal with the most important thing they possessed . . . this
mushy potato. I don't know who got the best of it—the mushy potato had
become joint property. They cooked it and stuffed it with whatever was avail-
able, threw a pastry dough around it and, Voilà, from this came a Potato Knish,
which means in Irish, Polish, and Lithuanian, "Mashed up with something
around the outside . . . altogether."*

*Their business was successful. They sold millions of Knishes and bought prop-
erty in the potato fields near Flatbush and Brooklyn Avenue in New York—near
the corner of Rodeo and Wilshire in Beverly Hills (then known affectionately as
"the hills"). You know the rest . . . their kids went into the movie business.*

*A couple of Knishes like the ones made from this recipe could get you
a screen test. Try it.*

INGREDIENTS, Serves 6 – 8

3 cups	**Flour**
I teaspoon	**Salt**
1/2 cup	**Vegetable Oil**

3/4 cup	**Lukewarm Water**
2	**Eggs,** beaten
4 cups	**Real Mashed Potatoes**
3 cups	**Onions,** grated and sauteed
2 tablespoons	**Butter,** melted
1/2 teaspoon	**Salt**
1/2 teaspoon	**White Pepper**
1 tablespoon	**Vegetable Oil,** to grease baking pan

METHOD

■ Combine flour and salt in a large bowl. Stir in oil, water and eggs to make dough. Knead for 5 minutes on a floured surface. Roll out into 4 inch squares about 1/8 to 1/4 inch thick.

■ Meanwhile in another bowl combine cooked potatoes, sauteed onions, butter, salt and pepper. Mix well.

■ Scoop out 4 ounces of potato mixture and place on top of dough squares. Pull the ends over top to cover the potato knish, brush with egg wash. Place in 350°F oven and bake for 30 minutes.

Meat Loaf

*Y*ou come home from your honeymoon, to your new apartment, all fresh and excited, your bride smiling and fussing in the kitchen. She knows what you have to do. You know. Perhaps you can delay a day or two, but no more.

The first day you're waiting for **The Call**. The phone is silent. You stare at it. The next morning it rings. There it is. **The Call**.

It's **Mom**. "We were waiting for your call, dear. We thought **you** would call us when you returned. Dinner next Saturday night? We miss you, you know. By the way, how is . . ." pregnant pause, "Barbara."

There are no choices. Saturday comes. It takes both of you about three hours to decide what to wear and get it all put together. Not too fancy, not too casual.

By the time you sit down to dinner the entire known world is a total nervous wreck. But the dinner smells sensational.

Mom brings out the main course. Meat Loaf. Her special recipe. You know it's wonderful. You know no one else in the whole world can make Meat Loaf like mama. And the gravy! Light, not sticky, delicate pieces of mushrooms floating in it.

Your mother grins like the proverbial Cheshire Cat. She knows. Your father knows. Your mom has got you. Meat Loaf and Moms. They never let go. Your wife pipes up. "This is so wonderful . . . Mom. Do you think I could have the recipe?"

Ha-ha-ha-ha-haa-ho-ho-haa-haa-haaa! Is this girl kidding??
Never!!

■ ■ ■ ■ ■

INGREDIENTS, Serves 6 – 8

I tablespoon	**Olive Oil**
I cup	**Carrots,** diced
1/3 cup	**Celery,** diced
I	**Onion**
1/2 cup	**Morel Mushrooms (optional)**
I clove	**Garlic,** minced or chopped
1/4 cup	**Beef Consumè** (or 1/2 cube of beef bouillon in 1/4 cup water, dissolved)
I pound	**Ground Beef** (15% fat)
1/2 pound	**Ground Pork**
1/2 pound	**Ground Veal**
I teaspoon	**Rosemary,** fresh or dried
I teaspoon	**Thyme,** fresh or dried
I	**Egg**

¹/₂ cup	**Cracker Crumbs** (or ¹/₄ cup each of Cracker Crumbs and Oatmeal, adding a touch extra salt if using oatmeal)
1 teaspoon	**Salt**
1 teaspoon	**Ground Pepper**
¹/₂ cup	**Tomato Sauce and a bit of A-1,** mixed in.
¹/₂ cup	**Red Wine**

METHOD

■ Heat oil in medium sauce pan over high heat.

■ When oil is good and hot, add carrots and cook until dark (not until night-time, silly—just until the carrots turn brown).

■ Reduce heat and add celery, toss and cook 3 minutes.

■ Add onions and mushrooms and cook another 3 minutes.

■ Add garlic and cook another minute or so.

■ Add half of the beef consumè and the wine. Blend. Remove from heat.

■ In large mixing bowl combine all meats and squeeze into one consistency. No chunks, please. You're not supposed to enjoy this squeezing business!

■ Add the cooked veggies and the rosemary and thyme to the meat, stir and squeeze.

■ Add the egg—after you've broken and blended it. Mix whole huge blob together thoroughly.

■ Add bread crumbs and oatmeal bit by bit, blend and toss in the salt and pepper.

■ Place the whole thing into an appropriate baking dish about 2 – 3 inches deep.

■ Spread tomato sauce and A-1 mixture over top.

■ Bake at 350° for about 1¹/₄ hours to 1¹/₂ hours.

■ Remove and let stand a few minutes. Slice and spread heated remaining consumè over slices. If you want, cook a few shallots and toss around the edges of the serving dish with some parsley.

Your wife tells your Mother that this was her own Moma's recipe. What a beginning!

Rice Pudding

*I*n the rice growing province of **Sin Ka Sip** deep in the heart of Communist China lives Mao Tse Pu Ding, a direct descendant of **Tse No Mo-Pe th'Goi**, a famous provincial warlord who refused to let anyone speak in his presence. **Tse No Mo** was ecstatic when his son, **Pu Ding** was born. He ordered up a huge feast but was at a loss for a good dessert since all they had was rice and because no one dared to tell him what to do with it.

Tse No Mo-Pe th'Goi searched long and hard for a celebration dessert. Years passed. Pu Ding grew into manhood. **Tse No Mo-Pe th'Goi** built an enormous kitchen for his chefs and went off to war leaving his beloved **Mao Tse Pu Ding** in charge. One day **Pu Ding** received news of his father's victories, the conquest of three mountain villages and a bus stop in Tibet at a minimal cost of four thousand dead and three thousand horses. **Pu Ding** created this dessert for the victorious homecoming.

The celebration didn't quite come off as **Tse No Mo-Pe th'Goi** died from an attack of gastroenteritis on the way home resulting from a bean and curd diet while on the road. Nevertheless, **Pu Ding's** recipe for this dessert remains— which, contrary to Communist dogma, was named after him.

Here it is from East of the Sun and West of the Moon.

■ ■ ■ ■ ■

INGREDIENTS, Serves 5 – 6

1/2 cup	**Long Grain Rice,** quick cook variety is OK
3 cups	**Milk** (2% fat is ok, but regular is better)
1/2 cup	**Sugar**
2	**Eggs**
1 teaspoon	**Vanilla Extract**
1/2 teaspoon	**Almond Extract**
1/2 cup	**Raisins**
1/2 cup	**Whipping Cream**

METHOD

■ Blend uncooked rice and milk together and cook so that rice is very soft. Add touch more milk if necessary.

■ Separate eggs. Beat egg yolks and stir into rice mixture.

■ Add vanilla and almond extracts. Mix.

■ Simmer again about 3 to 5 minutes. Remove from heat.

■ Beat egg whites until stiff and fold into pudding. Add sugar and fold into pudding.

■ Fold raisins into pudding. Let cool.

■ Beat whipping cream and then fold into pudding.

■ Spoon pudding into parfait glasses. Place in fridge.

■ Serve cold with small amounts of fresh fruit on top.

Bread Pudding

To have raisins or not have raisins, that is, indeed the question. Whether it's nobler, gentler, kinder and otherwise more commercial to have raisins in your bread pudding or not is the key philosophical inquiry for all "Deli-Cookers."

Henry VIII was convinced that raisins were required. Marie Antoinette believed they were an unnecessary luxury not due the masses. You know what happened to her. Do you recall that fateful evening in December in ancient times when Hamlet strode down the stairs into the great castle hall and ate a spoonful of his step-father's bread pudding? He hated his step-father. Remember? "Ugh!" he said to the false king who had murdered his father and deceived his mother, "No raisins! Dear God, no raisins!," and proceeded to kill the sonofabitch.

You know the rest . . . everyone dies. Including Hamlet. Who knew the bread pudding was poisoned? Which goes to show you what can happen if bread pudding doesn't have raisins.

INGREDIENTS, Serves 6 – 8

6 slices	**White Bread,** day old
2 tablespoons	**Butter** (or margarine)
1/2 cup	**Sugar**
1 teaspoon	**Cinnamon**
1/2 cup	**Raisins**
4	**Eggs**
2 cups	**Milk,** 2% fat OK
1 teaspoon	**Vanilla Extract**

METHOD

- Preheat oven to 350°F. Butter up a casserole dish, a one quart size will do best.
- Cut crusts off bread. Brush bread with melted butter or margarine on both sides. Sprinkle with sugar and cinnamon. Cut into quarters. Layer into baking dish and sprinkle each layer with raisins.
- In a bowl beat eggs and stir in milk, vanilla and remaining sugar. Stir until sugar dissolves.
- Pour over bread and raisins. Let soak.
- Set baking dish into larger pan containing about an inch of hot water.
- Bake an hour at 325°F. It's done when a knife inserted comes out clean.
- Can be served warm or placed into fridge and served cold.

This recipe can be made with egg bread. Many like it better with egg bread although not quite traditional American midwest.

Pot Roast and Potatoes

*T*he symbolism of a pot roast stewing in a luscious gravy with sweet onions and beautiful orange carrots and creamy colored little potatoes, looking like a Rembrandt masterpiece, a couple of bay leaves filling the kitchen with a kind of fresh breeze, is like the meaning of life itself. If there is a pot roast in your life every now and then, the sun is bright, nights are balmy, you are deliciously at ease, the evenings hold special promises, the bills are all paid, your mother isn't nagging, your dad thinks you're OK, your spouse smiles little whoopee smiles, everything is right with the world

A pastrami on rye, a mile high, with a ton of mustard and with no one watching as you try to clamp your mouth over one end might be the closest moment to the exquisite joy of watching a simmered pot roast and accoutrements dished out onto your plate.

The nicest words of the month are, "There's more, dear, if you want." There are some people sufficiently unbalanced never to order this dish. But we know . . . they are defined by their deficiencies—no pot roast, no love, no life, no balance.

We are giving you *b a l a n c e*. We are giving you *l o v e*. We are providing *j o y* in a joyless world. We are not charging enough for this book.

INGREDIENTS, Serves 6–8

I can	**Beer**
1/3 cup	**Strong Coffee** (European blend, freshly brewed)
I cup	**Beef Stock**
Smidgen	**Vinegar**
I teaspoon	**Brown Sugar** (preferred)
2	**Bay Leaves**

2 small cloves	**Garlic**
1/2 teaspoon	**Thyme**
Smidgen	**Allspice**
Smidgen	**Salt**
Smidgen	**Peppercorns**
1 tablespoon	**Olive Oil**
1 4 - 5 pound	**Chuck Roast,** center cut
2 - 3 teaspoons	**Margarine**
4 medium	**Onions,** sliced or diced
8 - 10 small	**Red Potatoes**
4 medium	**Carrots,** sliced or diced
1/4 cup	**Cold Water**
2 teaspoons	**Corn Starch**
1/4 cup	**Italian Parsley,** chopped

METHOD

■   In large bowl mix beer, coffee, beef stock, vinegar, sugar, bay leaves, garlic, thyme, allspice, salt and peppercorns, set aside.

■   Brown or sear meat in hot oil in a large stewing pot. Remove and place on platter. Retain oil.

■   Melt margarine in the stewing pot and add onions and potatoes. Saute until onions and potatoes show a little color. If potatoes are small leave whole.

■   Return meat to pan and add the bowl of condiments and carrots.

■   Cover and start to simmer for about 2 hours.

■   Remove meat for a minute or two while you blend the corn starch and water into the mixture in pan. Simmer and stir 1 - 2 minutes. Return meat.

■   Add parsley.

■   Invite relatives.

All sorts of things are optional here. More peppercorns or less, more or less potatoes. You can cut potatoes in half if you like. You can use less coffee, no more. A little paprika. A trifle more vinegar might add something which suits you. Suggest you do not use a strong beer or ale.

Stuffed Cabbage

Max and Morris are brothers and are childhood friends of my father. I know Morris real well but not Max who I never see because he lives at the race track. At least I think he does. I am twenty-five and looking to make my way in the world and I know Morris is rich, but I don't know about Max.

One day I visit Morris at his club to pick up a check for a little deal I made. Morris is playing bridge. At the next table, maybe twenty feet away, I see Max who I haven't seen in a long time and who might not recognize me. I ask Morris, "Would Max be interested?"

Morris looks up. Six wrinkled bridge players look up. I think I see a half dozen faint knowing smiles. Morris takes out a twenty dollar bill with a flourish, smacks it onto the table and says, "Kid, Max wouldn't give you the time of day! Go try."

I go over and introduce myself and Max remembers me and nods, barely looking up. He murmurs an inquires about my Father and my Aunt Nettie who he had a crush on in 1951, could have been '41, and nods again and returns to his game. I shuffle a little and finally ask, "Max, my watch is off, do you have the time?" He turns his head ever so slightly, his eyes flutter, his chin hardens, he is suddenly made from stone. "No, sorry, kid, I don't have the time."

Morris and the gang at the other table plotze. One big simultaneous gut busting plotze. Morris puts the twenty back into his pocket. "The time is one-thirty, kid, but you don't get the money."

*Have you ever tried to get a Stuffed Cabbage recipe from a friend, from **anyone**, without paying for it, or getting it out of a book?—same thing. Can't be done. There's a twenty on the table waiting for you. Try it. when you lose, the real thing is right here, also waiting for you.*

━━━ ■ ■ ■ ■ ■ ━━━

INGREDIENTS, Serves 6

1 large	**Cabbage,** green
2 teaspoons	**Salt**
1/4 - 1/2 pound	**Margarine**
1 cup	**Onions** white or yellow, diced
1 clove	**Garlic,** crushed
1/2 pound	**Mushrooms,** Sliced (try black porcini's)
1/2 pound	**Ground Beef**
1/2 pound	**Ground Veal**
1 1/2 cups	**White Rice,** cooked
3	**Hard Boiled Eggs,** chopped
1/4 cup	**Flour,** unsifted
1 can (6 oz.)	**Tomato Paste**
Smidgen	**Ground Black Pepper**
1/4 teaspoon	**Allspice**

METHOD

- Bring 6 cups of water to boil in a large saucepan.
- Add cabbage and 1 teaspoon salt, simmer 3 minutes.
- Drain, **keep** 2 cups of liquid.
- Remove 12 outer approximately equal sized leaves from cabbage.

Stuffing:

- Melt 1/4 cup margarine in large skillet. Toss in the onion. Saute until golden, but before totally limp.
- Add remaining margarine (not quite 1/4 pound) with garlic and mushrooms and saute about 4 minutes. Remove from heat.
- Add ground beef, veal, rice and hard boiled eggs. Mix it all up and and how about that?—Stuffing!
- Fill cabbage leaves with stuffing. Don't overdo. Fold 2 sides and then roll. Arrange rolls in large casserole dish, **seam side down**.

Tomato Sauce:

- Preheat the oven to 350°F.
- Melt 1/4 cup margarine in a medium saucepan. Remove from heat.
- Stir in flour into sauce pan. Blend smooth. Gradually stir in remaining cabbage liquid. Be gentle. Bring to boil.
- Remove from heat. Stir in tomato paste, salt, pepper and allspice.
- Pour sauce over rolls.
- Bake 25 minutes.

This is major cooking. You need the boss and his fussy wife and your social butterfly sister and her dentist husband to dine with you for this. Steamed green beans with a little vinegar in steaming water and butter patties and bacon bits tossed over when done is a good touch with this dish. I like sliced beef steak tomatoes tossed with red onion bits in wine vinegar and teaspoon olive oil and touch of ground pepper as starters. Colorful, too.

Corned Beef and Cabbage

*T*he exalted state of Good Judgment comes only from experience. Unfortunately, experience comes from bad judgments over a very long period of time. This rule is the major Catch 22 of life. You can't have anything worth having unless your path to it is strewn with the wreckage of your attempts. It is also true that every young person on the road to Good Judgment is positive that he or she has finally reached it with each attempt and just moments before the whole damn thing collapses from—bad judgments.

In other words you can't make a good corned beef unless you're past your fortieth birthday. Maybe more. You absolutely can't get any of the good things in life—grandchildren, medicare, social security, a bad temper, a big mouth—unless . . . you're older.

No wonder sensible women love experienced men and all men like experienced ballplayers and graying surgeons. Young people, when inviting special people over for dinner, do not generally serve corned beef and cabbage. It would not be their preference. That is because such uninitiated humans have not yet reached that exalted state of **Good Judgment**.

The creation of a good Corned Beef and Cabbage dish requires a delicate touch, a feel for timing, the intuitions of deep experience.

In short, you know what it needs.

INGREDIENTS,   Serves 6 – 8

4 – 5 pounds	**Corned Beef Brisket**
1 medium	**Garlic Clove**
1 medium	**Onion** (yellow onion preferred)
2	**Whole Cloves**
10	**Whole Black Peppercorns**
2	**Bay Leaves**
1/4 teaspoon	**Mustard Seed**
1 teaspoon	**White Wine Vinegar**
6 medium	**Carrots,** cut in 2 - 3 inch sections
1 medium head	**Green Cabbage,** cut in wedges

METHOD

■ Wipe corned beef with damp towels and place in large kettle. Cover with cold water. Toss all the remaining ingredients into the kettle except the carrots and cabbage. Bring to a boil, reduce heat, simmer about 5 minutes. Skim top.

■ Simmer for and additional 3 – 4 hours, covered. Skim top occasionally.

■ Half an hour before simmering is finished add the carrots .

■ Just before dinner, or last 15 minutes, cut cabbage into wedges and add.

■ Remove corned beef, cabbage and carrots from kettle. Slice beef against the grain. Arrange on a plater with the cabbage wedges and pieces of carrots for color.

Potato Pancakes

*O*nce upon a time, a handsome Prince kissed a really smashing looking commoner, named Geraldine, and a whole business erupted . . . What a ruckus! You can't kiss anyone without causing a ruckus if you're a Prince.

All the King's men were stumped. Does he marry this Commoner? Do they just give her a key to his back door or him a key to her back door, or build her a new house with a secret entrance? Do they give her a hairdo at Cristo's or take her like she is? Does her mother have all her teeth? What does her father do for a living? It's not like these questions aren't problems. There are other Kings and Princes to think about. And armies and Generals and ethnic considerations.

Then something happened. Her mother brought the King a sample of her locally famous potato pancakes. The King took a bite. The Prime Minister took a bite. The Queen hesitated and frowned and the King banished her immediately. Then the Prince took a bite. His face lit up. The King's face lit up. The Prime Minister's face lit up. Too much red pepper! They were about to lop off the head of Moma when Geraldine ran up to the Prince and kissed him real good and the Prince sort of melted. Moma pulled out another one of her potato pancakes and put it to the lips of the Prince. He tasted it and it was perfect. Geraldine and the Prince married. They might have lived happily ever after. Who knows? Everyone lies.

Here it is. You can make your own Potato Pancakes fit for King, a Prince, a Prime Minister, and even a banished Queen.

INGREDIENTS, Serves 8 – 10

3 pounds	**Potatoes,** peeled
1 pound	**Onions,** peeled
1/2	**Lemon,** the juice of
2	**Eggs**
2 tablespoons	**Salt**
1 teaspoon	**White Pepper**
4 ounces	**Flour**
3 ounces	**Matzo Meal**
2 ounces	**Oil**

METHOD

■ Grind or grate the potatoes and onions together; toss with the lemon juice.

■ Place the grated potatoes and onions in a stainless-steel, or a glass bowl.

■ Add all the remaining ingredients, except the oil.

■ Heat 1/4 inch of oil in a frying pan.

■ Put the potato batter into the hot oil by level serving spoon. When the pancakes are golden brown, turn and brown the other side.

■ Serve with apple sauce and sour cream.

Short Ribs in a Pot

*J*oseph Shawnley is a large cattle rancher along the Texas-New Mexico border. His spread was maybe a thousand, maybe fifteen hundred acres in size. He was born with the thirteenth rib missing on his right side which saddled him with sort of an underarm golf swing every time he shook hands.

Because kids are naturally mean they started calling him "Short Rib Shawnley" by the time he was six years old. When I got to know him, nearly sixty years later he had the incongruous mixture of white stubble for a beard and indigo thick black hair over eyes as gray as an evening sky.

One day Short rib realized that someone was stealing his cows, rustling them, just like in the old west. Worse than that they rustled his two best breeding heifers, Matt and Jake. Short Rib went looking for the bad guys and late one night came upon an old ramshackle cabin with thirty of what he was sure were his cattle in the foothills about twenty miles from his ranch.

Well, he sneaked up on that cabin and recognized Matt and Jake and they recognized him. The mooing and blubbering was something fierce. Then Short Rib peered into the cabin window and saw two fellows drinking bottles of Heinekin Lager who were three or four sheets to the wind.

He attacked. I can't tell you the rest, because Short Rib always refused to tell me. You have to imagine the ruckus. Suffice it to say he got his heifers and his cattle back. My understanding is that the local undertaker had a profitable weekend. The next time I saw Short Rib Shawnley he had a large bandage rolled around his chest and explained he had lost the thirteenth rib on his **left** side. The look he gave me told me not to ask more.

So Short Rib got sort of evened out late in life and lost his golf swing. His family started calling him "Short Ribs" now that the missing ribs had evened him up.

Which brings us to this recipe. Short Ribs Shawnley developed it between his sixty-fifth and his seventieth year. We call it **Shawnley's Symphony in a Pot**.

INGREDIENTS, Serves 6 — 8

4 2–3 pound	**Short Ribs of Beef**
I gallon	**Water**
I large	**Yellow Onion,** diced
I 1/2 cups	**Celery,** diced
2 cups	**Carrots,** diced
2 tablespoon	**Salt**
I teaspoon	**Black Pepper**
2 cups	**Chicken Soup** (or I can broth)
I package	**Wide Noodles**
4	**Matzo Balls and/or 8 Kreplach**

METHOD

■ Place ribs, water, vegetables and seasonings in a very large pot. Bring to a boil and simmer for 1 to 1¼ hours or until ribs are tender. Skim as necessary.

■ Remove ribs from pot and place into a serving pot or dish.

■ Add chicken soup to the large cooking pot (you can add 1 teaspoon chicken bouillon if desired).

■ Cook wide noodles separately—starting them about 15 minutes before the ribs are done—cook the noodles separately in boiling salted water (about 8 minutes), drain and add to large cooking pot.

■ Add matzo balls and/or kreplach to cooking pot. Simmer another five minutes.

■ Serve ribs and soup and veggies in a large bowl with thick slices of french bread.

This is the ultimate Deli meal especially if you choose to add both matzo balls and kreplach.

Brisket Roast

Comes to cooking everyone's a critic. To prove it I took notes on everything that occurred at the last family dinner at our house. My wife made a brisket. The recipe in this book.

*During dinner my mother kept running into the kitchen to clean things up **before** anything, anything at all, got dirty. This demonstrated a high degree of trust in my wife's kitchen habits. My dad finally grabbed her and held her down with one hand while he kept smiling and eating with his free hand. I waited to see how he would cut his meat. While holding my mother and waving his fork, he gave us all a wondrous smile and said, "this is really—wonderful—isn't it, dear?"*

*She didn't reply, just gave him a **look**.*

My sister and brother-in-law's oldest son, age fourteen, said, "C'n I go to the Burger King around the corner now?"

My wife's father looked up and remarked, "Grandchildren should be seen and not heard until the age of forty-two." Then he smiled and said, "Boy, you can cut this brisket with a fork!" My wife beamed. I beamed.

But my mother kept mumbling, "We'll never get this place cleaned up."

My sister, dear soul, said, sort of with a question in her voice, "They cook this at the Deli don't they?—Is that where you got it?"

Everyone's a critic.

I pretended I didn't hear.

My wife was great. She squeezed my hand between slices and asked if anyone wanted thirds. My father was managing with one hand and my mother picked at the carrots and potatoes.

I chalked up the night as a test of the strength of my marriage. We do not, however, speak about brisket roasts or nephews or one another's mother.

INGREDIENTS, Serves 4 – 6

1 2½ -3 pound	**Brisket**
1 cup	**Mushrooms,** sliced
2 large	**Onions,** diced
½ cup	**Celery,** chopped
½ cup	**White Wine**
2 teaspoons	**Salt**
Smidgen	**Ground Pepper,** to taste

1	**Package Liptons Dry Soup** (optional)
2 cups	**Water**
1 8 ounce can	**Tomato Sauce**

METHOD

■ Heat large frying pan, spray bottom lightly with oil spray and sear meat on each side. Don't get carried away.

■ Put the seared brisket in large pot and add all of the ingredients except the tomato sauce. Bring to a boil.

■ Simmer covered about 1 to 1 1/2 hours, depending on size.

■ Remove brisket and place on cutting board and slice in eighth to quarter inch slices.

■ Neatly return sliced meat to a baking dish and spread onions and other vegetables from the pot over meat with about a cup of the remaining water from the pot. Add packaged onion soup if desired and spread.

■ Spread tomato sauce over the meat and vegetables.

■ Bake another 3/4 hour uncovered in a 300° oven.

■ Cover with foil and bake another 1/4 to 1/2 hour, until meat suits your tender tastes. Add water as necessary so that a very small amount remains at bottom of baking dish. Sprinkle with pepper.

Shingebiss

An Ojibwe Legend

Retold by Nancy Van Laan
Woodcuts by Betsy Bowen ❖

Houghton Mifflin Company

Boston

Glossary

(All words in Ojibwe are spelled phonetically.)

adizookan: a traditional story that is spiritually alive
bee-in: come in
bon-in: sit with me or leave me alone
chemaywe'ya: the way-back time
Chippewa: another name for the Ojibwe
Kabibona'kan: Winter Maker
ka-neej: friend
Kawasa nangwana nintagawa-tim-asi: By no means is it
　　possible for me to freeze him
manitou: a spirit or supernatural force
Ojibwe (oh-JIB-way): tribe of the Algonquin stock
Ok-ee kaweya: Not hardly can you do me in, my fellow man
Shingebiss (ZHING-gih-biss): diving bird; known as a
　　diving duck, the merganser swims underwater to
　　catch fish
Zeegwan: Spring

Moon of the Freezing-Over-of-the-Earth: November

Spirit Moon: December

Great Spirit Moon: January

Stingy Moon: February

Maple Sugar Moon: March

Introduction

The Ojibwe, known also as the Chippewa, learned how to adapt to the harsh climate of the Great Lakes and the surrounding region by closely watching the birds and animals to see how they survived. This Ojibwe legend tells how little Shingebiss, the merganser duck, found a way to overcome the cold and survive the winter.

The Ojibwe believe that every living thing imparts a sacred teaching. Shingebiss, also called the diver, teaches several lessons: the importance of conservation, resourcefulness, and perseverance. Shingebiss is actually a spirit teacher who can assume a human form at any given time. Thus, in this story, Shingebiss may look like a duck but behaves in some ways like a human. While it might seem odd to think of a duck living in a wigwam and sitting by a fire, it isn't for the Ojibwe. Transformation, the ability to change back and forth from animal or bird to man, is accepted by all native peoples.

Ojibwe stories are not like European fairy tales or fables, which were "human-made" and which served as a form of entertainment. The tales of the Ojibwe are alive like spirits, and have been passed down to each generation from *chemaywe'ya*, the way-back time.

He, Shingebiss, so bold and free,
Was duck or man, as he might please;
Him, in his barky wigwam, He,
Ka-bibono'ka, could not freeze;
But four small logs the winter through
Had he to burn to keep him warm;
Yet stout of heart, no fear he knew —
Laughed at the Winter's raging storm.

— Benjamin Hathaway, 1882

During the Moon of the Freezing-Over-of-the-Earth, when Winter Maker blows his icy breath across the land, all but the bravest birds fly south. Animals, both large and small, seek warmth wherever they can and often go hungry, for snow-covered ground and frozen waters make it hard to find enough to eat.

But there is one small being who faces the wind of the great Winter Maker, one who knows how to pluck fish out of frigid waters. It is Shingebiss, the diver, who once challenged Kabibona'kan, Winter Maker, in the way-back time.

It was in *chemaywe'ya*, the way-back time, that
Shingebiss lived in a wigwam made of bark, tucked
between tall pines.

His wigwam, small but cozy, rested near the waters of Great Lake Superior, which was full of fish for Shingebiss to eat.

During the warm months of spring and summer,
Shingebiss glided across the deep blue waters,
dipping here and there, catching minnows as they
skimmered near the surface.

When autumn chilled the air, Shingebiss could

dive below, swimming like a brook trout beneath
the waters. He could always find plenty to eat.
Even in winter, Shingebiss could fish, for Lake
Superior is much too large to freeze over, as most
lakes do.

But once during the Spirit Moon, the first moon of winter and of deep snow, the chilling breath of Kabibona'kan froze the waters of Great Lake Superior. Even a moose could now cross the vast lake without breaking the ice. It was as solid as stone.

In his lodge, Shingebiss had but four logs to keep him warm. Four logs, one for each cold winter month. He did not want to starve during this harsh season as so many others might. What he needed was a way to fish through the thick ice.

So, fearlessly, Shingebiss ventured outdoors to face the great wind of Winter Maker.

Kabibona'kan roared a warning: *"Whoooo-ish!* Go back inside, little duck. There is no food for you out here."

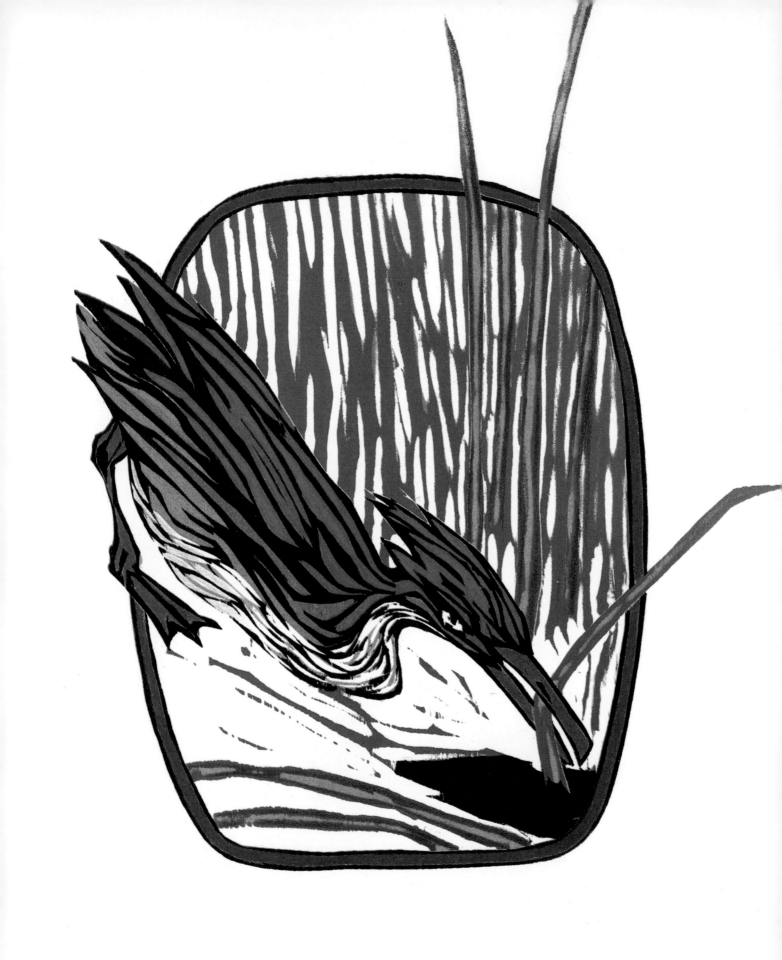

But Shingebiss was not afraid. Hardy and free, he set forth, *wa-wah, wa-wah*, down to the edge of the frozen lake. Slowly he made his way across the ice toward a patch of frozen rushes. He tugged on the tall stalks and yanked them up, making a hole in the ice just big enough for his small body. Quickly he dove through the opening and got fish for his supper. Then away to his lodge he went, *wa-wah, wa-wah*, dragging his fish behind him.

Inside his wigwam, with his first log burning brightly, Shingebiss ate his dinner.

Outside, Winter Maker roared and screamed beneath the first moon of winter. He did not like so small a being showing no fear. So his great wind blew and blew for many days, until deep drifts of snow covered the tiny wigwam. Shingebiss, hearing the great wind outside, moved closer to his fire for warmth.

After many days, the storm ended. Clever Shinge-biss used his webbed feet to dig a tunnel through the heavy drifts. After much work, he crawled up and out into the bright December morning. Happily he ruffled his feathers to shake off the snow, then set forth, *wa-wah, wa-wah,* down to the edge of the frozen lake. Just as before, he pulled up reeds, then dove into the hole to fish. And once again, he returned home with his fish trailing behind him.

However, all during the second moon of winter, the Great Spirit Moon, Shingebiss had no fish to eat. This time when Winter Maker howled and roared, he coated the deep snow with ice thicker than the trunk of an old cedar, ice so thick that Shingebiss was unable to break through it. All the while, Shingebiss grew hungrier and hungrier, with only the warmth of his second log to comfort him.

But finally one quiet morning, the ice storm left, and Shingebiss discovered that he could use his strong beak to peck through the ice. *Pik, pik, pik! Pik, pik, pik!* He hopped out of his wigwam, then hurried, *wa-wah, wa-wah,* down to the frozen lake. Again, he pulled up rushes, made a hole in the ice, dove in and, at last, brought fish home for his supper.

In his wigwam, he ate hungrily. Then he carefully placed his third log on the glowing coals. It was now the third moon of winter, the Stingy Moon, the tough month when all the animals hole up. No creature dared to venture outdoors during this time — not Bear or Skunk or Beaver — no creature except Shingebiss. He still caught his fish every day, cooked his supper every night, and warmed himself by the fire of his third log.

Seeing Shingebiss so brave and content made Winter Maker angrier than ever. So this time, instead of deep snow or thick ice, Winter Maker sent a chilling wind that raged for many days without stopping. The breath of this wind was so cold that it cracked the rocks and broke the trees. Even the animals who were safely holed up were shivering as they slumbered.

"Oooohh . . . Ahhh!" cried Kabibona'kan as his winds raged. "What kind of being are you?" he asked. "I will find a way to defeat you!"

But as soon as Shingebiss heard the winds die down, he walked, *wa-wah, wa-wah,* down to the frozen lake. As usual, he pulled up some reeds and prepared to dive through the opening in the ice. He did this not knowing that Winter Maker was right behind him.

See-whishhhhh! Kabibona'kan blew his icy breath over the hole. Instantly it closed up. Pretending that nothing had happened, Shingebiss quickly pulled up some other reeds, then dove through that hole.

"Ahhhhhhhh!" cried Winter Maker. "Now I've got you, little duck!" With another mighty huff of frigid air, he closed up the hole. "Stay down below, little duck! Stay below the frozen waters forever!"

But a few moments later, near the shore where a river current thins the ice, Winter Maker heard *Pik, pik, pik! Phit-phit-phit!*

Then several rushes disappeared under the ice. Up bobbed Shingebiss, with a mouthful of fish!

"Oh, no, *hey!"* said Kabibona'kan, so surprised that he only watched as the little duck returned, *wa-wah, wa-wah,* to his home, with a string of fish trailing behind him.

It was then that Kabibona'kan came up with a new plan. Now he would show the little duck just how powerful he could be. Slowly, quietly, Winter Maker crept up to the entrance of the wigwam. Shingebiss was just throwing on his last log, and this log had to burn all during the Maple Sugar Moon, until beautiful Zeegwan would arrive to warm the earth. It was Winter Maker's plan to cool the lodge so much that the fourth log would not last until spring. Then Shingebiss would freeze.

But Shingebiss, feeling Winter Maker's chilly breath come in through the cracks of the flap, knew who was there. So he sang:

> *"Ka-neej, ka-neej,*
> *Bee-in, bee-in.*
> *Bon-in, bon-in.*
> *Ok-ee, ok-ee.*
> *Ka-weya, ka-weya!"*

> (Friend, friend,
> Come in, come in.
> Sit with me
> Or leave me alone.
> You are but my fellow man;
> Not hardly can you do me in.)

This only enraged Kabibona'kan all the more, for he knew that the little duck was still not afraid of him.

So Winter Maker slipped silently under the door, rustled right behind little Shingebiss, and sat like an icicle, pale and cold, next to the fire.

Again Shingebiss sang:

"Ka-neej, ka-neej,
Bee-in, bee-in.
Bon-in, bon-in.
Ok-ee, ok-ee,
Ka-weya, ka-weya!"

Now the little lodge was growing very warm. And, as sparks from the last log shot up, Winter Maker's great body began to melt.

"Little duck, what kind of being are you?" he asked. "I have tried to freeze you. I have tried to starve you. But there you sit, hardy and free as though nothing could do you any harm."

As the last log glowed a deep red, tiny drops of water appeared on Kabibona'kan's face and filled his eyes of snow. His towering shape began to sag, and finally he said softly, "Shingebiss, you must be aided by some *manitou,* some great spirit. I cannot stand this. I must go out."

Little Shingebiss stood in the doorway and watched
as Kabibona'kan flung himself into a bank of deep
snow. Slowly, ever so slowly, Winter Maker grew

colder and colder until at last, when the Maple
Sugar Moon was bright and full, he was as great and
powerful as before.

In a blinding whirlwind of sleet and ice, Kabibona'kan rose up, eager to return to his home in the far north. It was almost the end of winter, and Zeegwan, Spring, would soon be claiming the land.

As he blew across the starlit sky, the thin night air echoed his words: *"Kawasa nangwana nintagawa-tim-asi.* I can neither freeze Shingebiss nor starve him; he is a very singular being. I will let him alone."

Kabibona'kan kept his promise.

Year after year, even in the coldest of months, Shingebiss continues to live out the winter by breaking through the ice and diving for fish.

Just as this story, this sacred *adizookan*, teaches, those who follow the ways of Shingebiss will always have plenty of fish to eat, no matter how hard the great wind of Winter Maker blows.

For my dear nephew, Jan Greven, whose skilled research and devotion to this little duck greatly enhanced this retelling. —N.V.L.

To my friends at Grand Portage. *Megwetch,* thanks. —B.B.

Illustrator's note:
The pictures in this book are woodblock prints, made by carving the design into a flat plank of white pine, rolling colored ink onto the block, and printing on a Vandercook No. 4 letterpress housed at the historic Grand Marais Art Colony. The cycle is repeated for each color, carving away more parts of the block, changing ink color, and printing again, five runs for each picture. This is called the reduction method. More colors are added later with colored pencils. The shape of the borders was inspired by the shape of the Ojibwe birchbark ricing baskets.

Sources
Tobacco and gifts were taken to an elder in the Grand Portage Chippewa Band to ask for an understanding of this story.

Emerson, Ellen Russell. *Indian Myths.* Minneapolis: Ross & Haines, 1965.
Hathaway, Benjamin. *The League of the Iroquois and Other Legends.* Chicago: S.C. Griggs and Company, 1882.
Johnston, Basil. *Ojibway Heritage.* New York: Columbia University Press, 1976.
Jones, William. *Ojibwa Texts.* Edited by Franz Boas. Volume VII, Part II. American Ethnological Society, 1919.
Schoolcraft, Henry R. *The Myth of Hiawatha and Other Oral Legends.* Philadelphia: Lippincott, 1856.
Williams, Mentor L., editor. *Schoolcraft's Indian Legends.* East Lansing: Michigan State University Press, 1956, 1991.

Text copyright © 1997 by Nancy Van Laan
Illustrations copyright © 1997 by Betsy Bowen

www.houghtonmifflinbooks.com

The text of this book was hand-lettered by the artist.
The illustrations are prints, created through the reduction process, reproduced in full color.

Library of Congress Cataloging-in-Publication Data
Van Laan, Nancy.
Shingebiss: an Ojibwe legend / retold by Nancy Van Laan ; woodcuts by Betsy Bowen.—1st ed.
p.   cm.
Summary: Shingebiss the duck bravely challenges the Winter Maker and manages to find enough food to survive a long, harsh winter.
RNF ISBN 0-395-82745-0   PAP ISBN 0-618-21616-2
1. Ojibwe Indians–Folklore. 2. Legends–Great Lakes Region. [1. Ojibwe Indians – Folklore. 2. Indians of North America – Great Lakes Region – Folklore. 3. Folklore – Great Lakes Region. 4. American merganser – Folkore. 5. Ducks – Folklore.]
1. Bowen, Betsy, ill. II. Title. E99.C6V35   1997   398.2'089973 – dc20 [E] 95-40274 CIP AC

Printed in the United States of America
BVG 10 9 8 7 6 5 4 3 2